Gabriela Popa

FOCUS YOUR MIND

Coloring Book

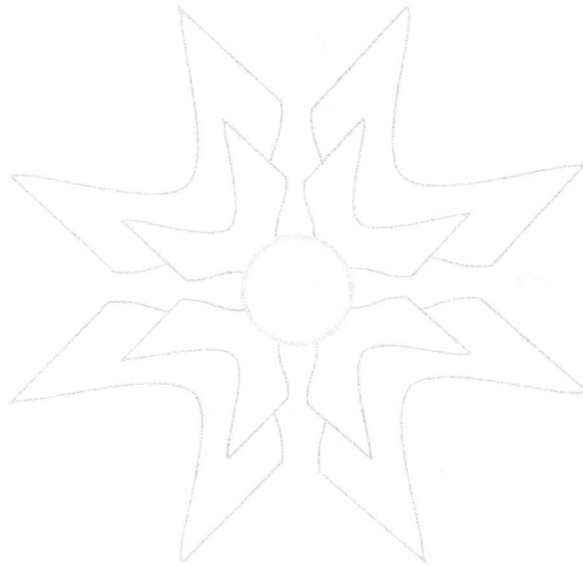

Published in 2015 by
Pixiphoria
St. Louis, MO

Copyright © 2015 Gabriela Popa

ISBN: 0983864136
ISBN-13: 978-0983864134

Printed in the United States of America

From the library of

_____

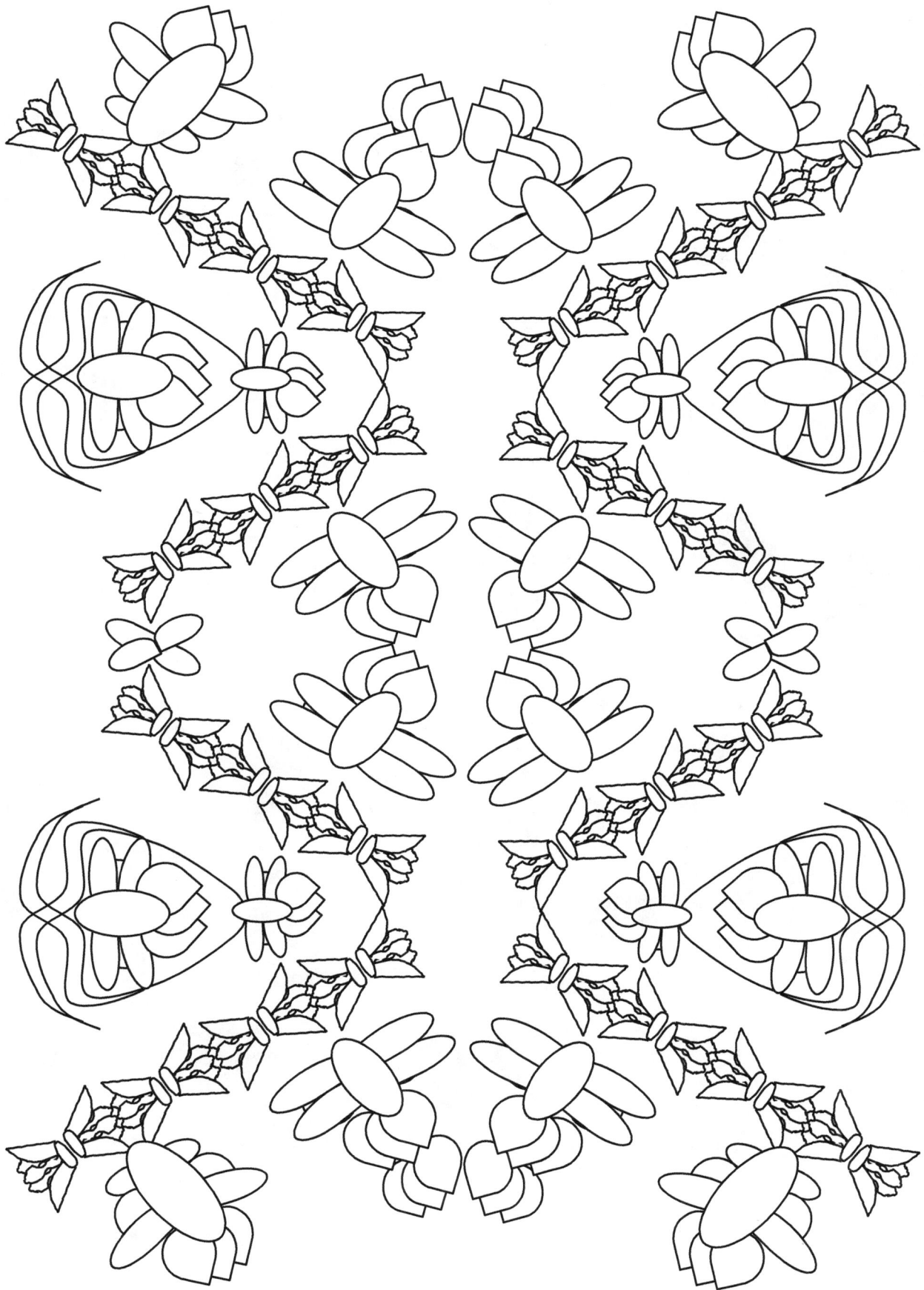

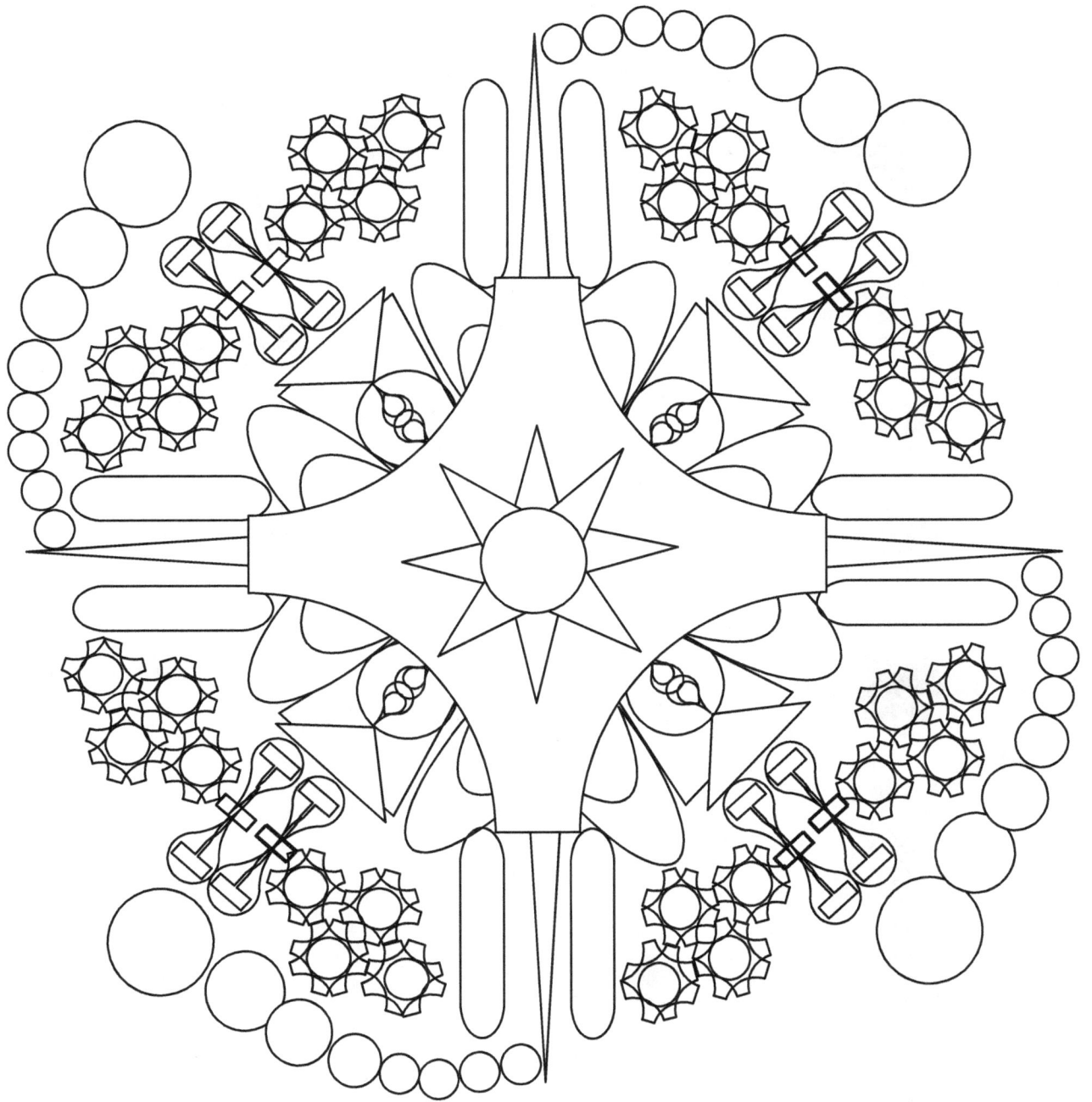

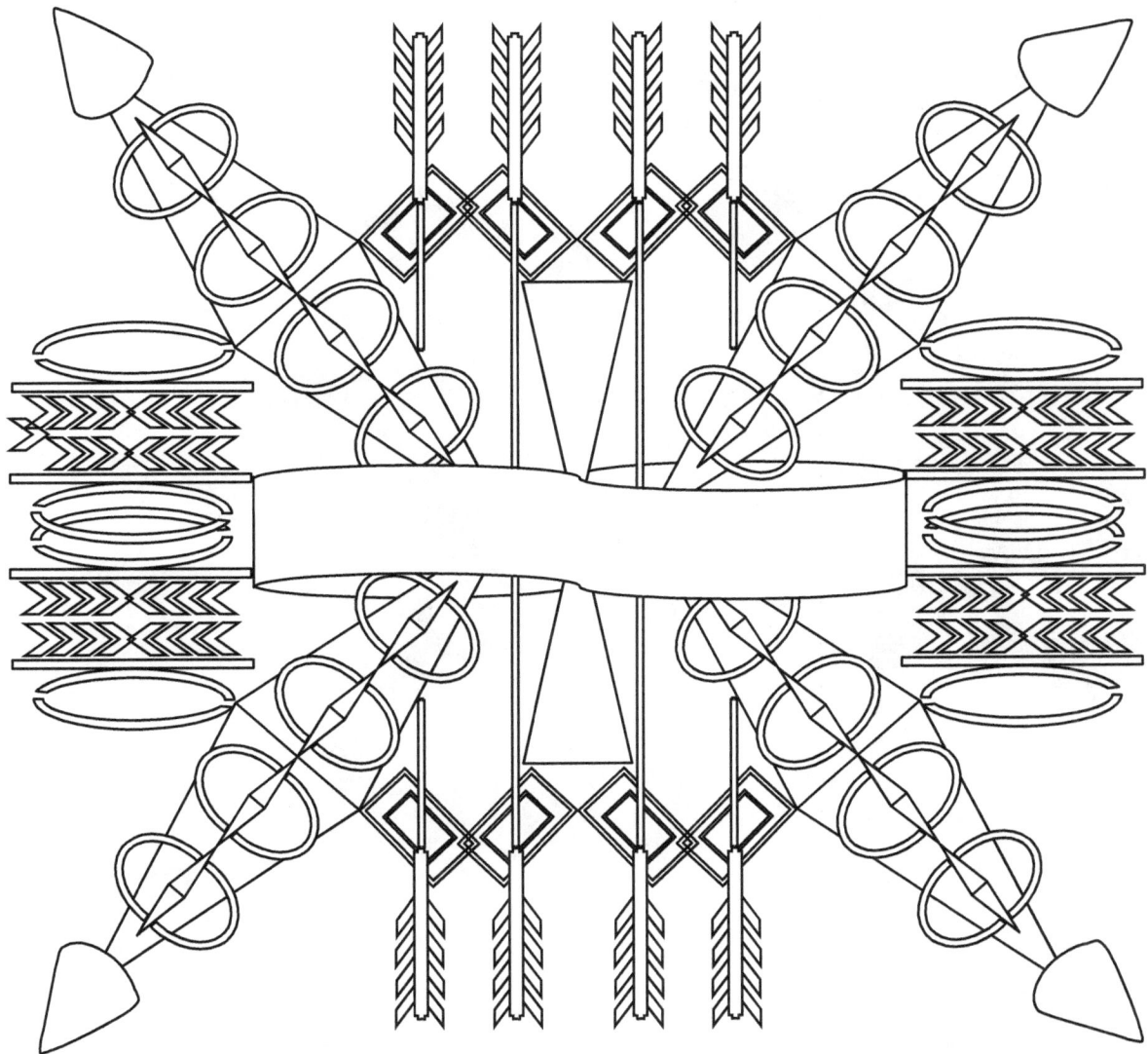

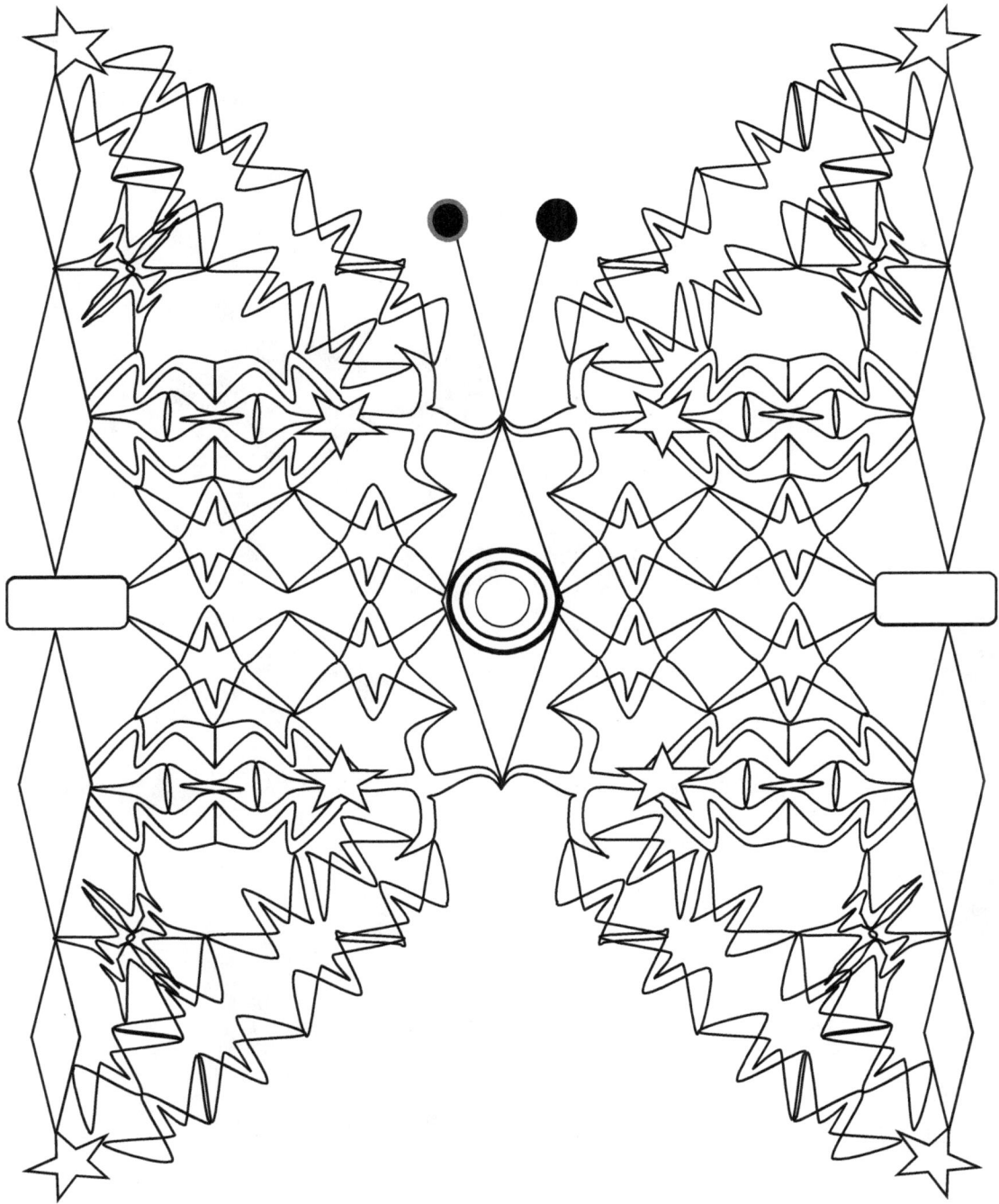

www.ingramcontent.com/pod-product-compliance
Lightning Source LLC
Chambersburg PA
CBHW080208300326
41934CB00038B/3409